on the open road

A NEW PLAY

STEVE TESICH

An Applause Original
ON THE OPEN ROAD

ISBN: 1-55783-134-3

APPLAUSE THEATRE BOOK PUBLISHERS
211 West 71st Street
New York, NY 10023
Phone: 212-496-7511, Fax: 212-721-2856

THE NEW YORK SHAKESPEARE FESTIVAL

Joanne Akalaitis, *Artistic Director*, Jason Steven Cohen, *Producing Director*, Rosemarie Tichler, *Associate Artistic Director*

presents

ON THE OPEN ROAD

Directed by
Robert Falls

Set Design by
Donald Eastman

Sound Score by
John Gromada

Costume Design by
Gabriel Berry

Production Stage Manager
Peggy Imbrie

Lighting Design by
Kenneth Posner

Dramaturg
Jason Fogelson

Casting by
Jordan Thaler

Al . . . . **Byron Jennings**
Angel . . . . **Anthony La Paglia**
The Little Girl. . . . . **Ilana Seagull**
The Monk . . . . **Henry Stram**
Jesus . . . . **Andy Taylor**
The Little Boy . . . . **Sean Nelson**

"ON THE OPEN ROAD" opened at The Joseph Papp Public Theater on February16, 1993.

World Premiere of **ON THE OPEN ROAD**
at THE GOODMAN THEATRE

Robert Falls, Artistic Director, Roche Schulfer, Producing Director

Directed
By
Robert Falls

Set Design
by
George Tyspin

Projections
by
John Boesche

Costume Design
by
Gabriel Berry

Production
Stage Manager
Joseph
Drummond

Lighting Design
by
Michael Phillipi

Sound Design
by
Rob Milburn

Stage Manager
T. Paul Lynch

Al . . . . **Jordan Charney**
Angel . . . . **Steve Pickering**
The Little Girl . . . . **Denisha Powell**
The Monk. . . . . **Christopher Pieczynski**
Jesus . . . . **Andy Taylor**
Boy . . . . **Somebody Else**

"ON THE OPEN ROAD" opened at The Goodman Theatre, Chicago, Illinois on March 16, 1992.

TIME: A time of Civil War

PLACE: A place of Civil War

ACT I

SCENE ONE

Exterior. Outskirts of some city. Day. Center stage, standing on an overturned trash can, is a man. His feet are tied around the ankles. His hands are tied behind his back. He wears a gag around his mouth and a professional-looking noose around his neck. The end of the rope is tied to something high over his head, a light fixture of some kind or a utility pole. The noose is tight and so is the rope. If he fell off the trash can, he would be hung. His name is Angel. He stands there, looking left, looking right, looking out.

Enter Al, stage right. He's smoking a cigarette butt. He's wearing glasses and he's pulling a cart. The cart has a tarp over it, so we can't see its contents, but we can tell by the way he's pulling it that the cart is heavy and that Al is very tired.

Al stops when he sees Angel. Looks him up and down and then all the way up to where the rope is attached. Starts moving again, pulling the cart, going past Angel.

Angel makes some noise. He's probably pleading for help, but we can't understand what he's saying because of the gag around his mouth. Nor does Al seem to care what he's saying. But the cart is heavy and Al is tired and it's a very hot day. Al stops again. Looks back at Angel. Looks long and hard at him, thinking, considering, weighing some possibility. Then he looks all around, as if checking for possible danger of some kind. Sensing none, he heads toward Angel. Stops. Goes back to cart. There's a ladder attached to the outside of the cart which he removes and carries with him. He spreads the legs of the ladder. Tests to make sure the ladder is steady. Climbs up the ladder until he's at roughly the same height as Angel.

Al: I might have a business proposition for you.

Angel nods emphatically and maybe adds some vocal affirmations which we can't understand.

I'm not promising anything, you understand. It all depends on the interview. If you're not used to interviews, here's a helpful hint: Just be yourself. If it works out, it works out. If it doesn't, it doesn't, right?

Angel nods and grunts a reply. Al takes out a knife from his jacket. Opens it. Likes the position he's in: A knife in his hand next to a man who's helpless. Plays with this for a second or so. Angel is clearly wondering what he plans to do with that knife.

Interviews work like this. I ask you a question and you reply. You don't speak unless I ask you to speak. Understand?

Angel nods. Al takes the blade of the knife. Puts the

point under the gag and then cuts it. The gag falls off.

Al: Now to business. Who left you here like this?

Angel: A lynch mob.

Al: Did you do something to provoke them?

Angel: Yes, I was alive when they came along.

Al: Why didn't they finish the job?

Angel: One of them suggested they set fire to me and then hang me. So they ran off to look for some kerosene. I don't know why they never came back.

Al: Whose side are you on?

Angel: You mean the Civil War?

Al: What else is there?

Angel: I've lost track of sides.

Al: Let us say you ran into Christian Democrats or Social Democrats, or Corporate Christians or National Socialists or the Blues or the Reds or the Whites or some splinter group of any of the above? Which of them would you be most likely to join?

Angel: If the King of Hell had a faction, I'd sign up if he'd set me free.

Al: So I guess at the moment you'd call yourself an Independent.

Angel: I'll call myself whatever you want to call me, Mister.

Al feels his biceps and chest.

Al: You seem pretty strong.

Angel: I'm even stronger when I'm not tied up.

Al: Do you have any special skills? Something you're good at?

Angel: I used to be a prize fighter before the Civil War broke out. If you need a bodyguard or something like that.

Al: I need an ox.

Angel: I'll do anything.

Al: Did you ever kill anybody?

Angel: Yes.

Al: Would you kill again?

Angel: Yes.

Al: Is there something you wouldn't do?

Angel: Can't imagine what it could be.

Al: What would you say if I said that you were the scum of the earth.

Angel: I'd say you know your scum, Mister.

Al: What is your name?

Angel: Angel.

Al: Mine's Al.

Angel: Pleased to meet you, Al.

Al cuts the ropes around Angel's ankles. Then he cuts his hands free. As soon as his hands are free, Angel hurriedly loosens, removes and throws away the noose.

Angel: Free again!

He comes toward Al with open arms. Al stops his advance with his knife.

Al: Back off.

Angel: I was just going to embrace you, brother.

Al: We'll skip the embrace.

Angel: Maybe you don't understand the true depth of my gratitude. See. I was tied up there for hours. Waiting to be hung. Waiting to be set on fire. To die. People went by. Saw me and just kept on going.

I gotta tell you, Al, I was beginning to lose faith in my fellow man. I wasn't just gonna die. I was gonna die depressed. And then you came along and saved me. See. you didn't just save my life. You saved me from the trap of pessimism into which I was falling. You have revived my faith in man, Al.

Al: Good for me. Now let's get going.

Angel: Wait a minute. Just tell me, what was it about me that made you stop? I mean, you must have seen something in me to go through all the trouble of saving my life. What was it?

Al: I needed somebody to pull my cart. A human ox, that's what I saw.

Angel: Don't give me that. You know and I know that I gave a rotten interview and still you took me on. So what was it, Al? What did you see in me?

Al: There's the cart. Start pulling.

Angel obeys. He lifts up the tarp, curious to see

what's inside.

Angel: What's all this?

Removes the tarp some more for a better look. Inside we see priceless paintings. The cart's full of them.

Where did you get all this stuff?

Al: Bombed out museums. Ransacked mansions of the rich. I follow the mobs.

He puts the tarp over the cart again.

C'mon. Let's get going.

Angel:

Gets ready to pull. Stops.

Where're we going?

Al: Have you ever heard of the Land of the Free?

Angel: Who hasn't?

Al: That's where I'm going.

Angel: I hate to pop your bubble, brother, but I don't think they let people like us in there anymore.

Al: I know. But maybe I know of a way.

Angel: Holy shit. I not only get saved, but I get saved

by a guy with a plan. Is that what you got, Al? You got a plan to sneak into the Land of the Free?

Al: Maybe.

Angel: That's what you saw in me, wasn't it? A man who, although he looks like the scum of the earth on the outside, could blossom like a fucking flower in the Land of the Free, right?

Al: Yeah, right.

Angel comes toward him with open arms.

Angel: Let me embrace you, brother.

Al: I said, we'll skip the embrace, scum.

Angel: Sorry. I come on too strong, right? I know. But I understand your position. Let's not rush things, right? Right, I know. True friendship takes time. We'll do it your way. We'll get to know each other slowly, and then slowly but surely we'll open up our hearts to one another and . . .

Al has been listening impatiently but, sensing that Angel just intends to go on, he slaps him.

Al: Stop that drivel.

Angel, a born fighter, is ready to deck him, but checks himself.

Angel: You know, I'll tell you something. I take this as a good sign. If you can feel comfortable enough around me to biff me one, for my own good probably, that you care enough in the first place to biff me one for my own good already shows me that you and I are gonna . . .

Al: If we must speak to each other . . .

Angel shuts up.

as I see we must, let's get something cleared up right at the start. Men like you are born by the metric ton every day and if I have any feelings toward you, it's out of sheer fascination that somebody with a brain the size of a cigarette butt can even function.

Angel: Nobody's ever taken the trouble to talk straight to me like that and I'll tell you something, Al, I for one appreciate it. There can be no true friendship without honesty and the fact that you already feel free to be honest around me already shows me . . .

Al: LIKE I SAID. If we must speak to each other, then we will at least try and confine ourselves to speaking of things that matter. And since you haven't a clue what those things are, I will teach them to you. In return for your manual labor, I will be your mentor and I'll try to elevate your mind along the way. We'll start with classical music. Pay attention. I'll quiz you later. We'll begin with the grail motif from *Parsifal*, by Richard Wagner.

Al vocalizes the grail motif and leads the way.

Angel, pulling the cart, follows. They exit.

Blackout.

SCENE TWO

Out of the darkness, a ray of light illuminates a large beautiful statue. The statue is still for a beat or so and then it begins to rise up. More light. We now see that we're inside a large bombed-out museum. A thick, nylon rope is attached to the statue. The rope is draped over a high steel beam overhead, exposed by the bombing. Using a pulley, Angel is lifting the statue off the ground. The cart is not far away. Al has taken off the tarp and is now taking out some paintings that we can't see. He is stacking them on the ground to make room for the statue. More light. We see little pyramids of dead bodies here and there. Corridors radiating in three directions. Angel grunts as he works. Despite the pulley, it's hard work lifting up the statue. When it's high enough, Al will position the cart to receive the statue and Angel will lower it. Once in the cart, Al will wedge in the paintings around it and Angel will disassemble the pulley and put the rope and the pulley in the cart and Al will then place the tarp over the whole thing and the cart will be ready to go. All this will take place during Angel 's monologue.

Angel: If I was God, I'd change some things in the Bible. About how you shouldn't make graven images of God. If I was God, I wouldn't give a shit if they made graven images of me. What do I care? I'm God. Can't hurt me to be graven. Nothing can hurt me. I'm God. But I would put in its place, in big letters: Thou shalt not make graven images of your fellow man.

He pauses to rest a bit.

You know Al, The very first time I ever went to a museum was right before the Civil War broke out.

Continues to work.

It was one of those scum-of-the-earth days at the museum. If you're scum, you get in free. These social agencies rounded us up and took us there in school buses. About three hundred of us. Young scum. Old scum. Half-way house scum. No-house scum. A cross-section. It was in order to uplift us they took us there. I was delighted to be in that air-conditioned place. That by itself was uplifting enough for me.

The statue is now high enough. Al moves the cart under it. Angel lowers it slowly, as Al guides it.

But there was this exhibit there in the museum. These artworks of a socially conscious nature. And every work of art showed some man or woman or kid who was having a real bad time of it. Street-type sufferers and the like. We're snickering among ourselves in that stupid scum-of-the-earth way of ours. What? We came all the way here to see more scum like us. But the others, the regular people, in chic lightweight summer suits and dresses with brochures in their hands, they're not snickering at all. And they're offended 'cause we are. They are seriously moved by what they see in the exhibit. They are telling each other how beautiful it all is, this exhibit of human suffering. I try to ignore them, but it was like the air-conditioning broke down or something, 'cause I start feeling hot. It's rubbing me all wrong to hear about the beauty of it all. Not that far from the museum, twenty blocks or so uptown where I lived, there was the same kind of exhibit. Same kind of suffering. Only it wasn't beautiful there. And there were no couples in chic lightweight summer clothes to be moved by it all. What was fucking scum-of-the-earth outside the museum was a fucking masterpiece inside. And then this thing starts crawling through my brain. This really painful idea that maybe there was something in me worth seeing, that nobody would ever see so long as these artworks were there. I know what I'm thinking, but I'm trying not to think it, 'cause it's no good thinking such thoughts. But then I hear it. It's like I hear the other scum-of-the-earth there thinking the same thing. And suddenly it's a much bigger thought. It's like ants. I read in this nature magazine once that ants don't have brains and that ants don't talk unless there's enough of them that get together. Two ants got nothing to say to each other. They don't know what to do. But if a few hundred of them get together, a brain is born. Suddenly, we started trashing it all. Breaking up statues and tearing the paintings to shreds. There were these armed guards there and they shot a bunch of us, but we didn't care.

Ants don't really care if a bunch gets killed. We set fire to the museum and ran out into the street.

The cart is loaded. The tarp is over the cart. The ladder now hangs from some pegs on its side.

Al: And so another Civil War began.

Angel: For once I was there at the start of something. It was very pleasant to realize you didn't really have to be highly qualified to make history.

Al: Merely stupid.

Angel: That's what was so nice. The feeling that being stupid was not a handicap for a change. Now, of course, I'm all confused. I mean, here I am wandering around with you, trying to salvage the very things I set out to destroy.

Al: You've come full circle. The very things you wanted to destroy are the only things that can save you now. As I told you, people like you come in bulk. And they don't let refugees into the Land of the Free by the metric ton anymore. You have to be culturally qualified to get in.

Angel: Live and learn, right, Al? Live and fucking learn. I thought it was the culture that was oppressing me. Wrong. It's culture that's gonna liberate me.

Al interrupts him.

Al: Shhh!

Angel: What?

Al: Listen.

Both listen. A faint sound of a 'male chorus', singing. It should be something from the archives of Hitler Jugend. Both run to where they can get a look at who's approaching.

Angel: Who the fuck are they?

Al: I don't think they're a band of wandering troubadors. Let's get the hell out of here.

The song gets louder as they hurry to exit. The cart is much heavier now and Angel has to struggle to pull it. They exit. The song gets louder and louder.

Blackout.

The song continues in the darkness and then stops.

SCENE THREE

On the road. Al is leading. Angel is pulling the cart. A body of a man lies on the ground.

Angel: I'm hungry.

They go past the body on the ground without so much as a glance at it.

Angel: I'm starved.

But something catches Al's eye about the body. He stops. Goes back and takes a closer look. The man is lying on his stomach. His arms are stretched out and his hands are clutching a small rectangular tin container. It's the container that caught Al's eye. It's the container he examines.

Al: Would you look at this?

Angel: What is it?

Al: It's a tin of petite beurres.

Angel: What's that?

Al: Euro-cookies. Delicious, firm. Made with butter.

Angel: Oh yeah!

He drops the cart and rushes toward the tin. Al has to push him away before he can get his hands on it.

Al: What do you think you're doing?

Angel: I'm hungry. I want some of those cookies.

Al: So am I. And so do I. But we can't have any.

Angel: We can't! Why not?

Al: Scruples.

Angel: What scruples?

Al: My scruples. Or rather my scruple. I'm down to one last solitary scruple. But times being what they are one scruple is all I need to feel morally superior to the rest of mankind. I like feeling morally superior. Unfortunately my last remaining scruple prevents me from robbing the dead.

Angel: You gotta be kidding. You mean we can't yank that tin of cookies out of that stiff's hands?

Al: I don't see how we can if I'm to remain morally superior.

Angel: It's too fucking bad you picked that particular scruple to keep.

Al: It's tragic. I love petite beurres.

Angel: I have an idea.

Al: What?

Angel: I don't have any scruples that I'm aware of.

Al: Oh, that. I've already thought of that. You mean

you could pry the tin from the corpse.

Angel: It would be my pleasure. And if because of your scruple you can't bring yourself to eat any of the cookies . . . I'll understand. You'll still be morally superior and I won't be so hungry, what do you say?

Al: Impossible. You see, as your mentor, I cannot condone in you what I would condemn in myself. The price of moral superiority is consistency.

Angel: Hunger is a heavy price to pay for moral superiority.

Al: That's why I'm down to only one scruple.

Angel: I have an idea.

Al: Two in one day!

Angel: What if he wasn't dead?

Al: My scruple only covers the dead. If he were alive we could rob him at will.

Angel: That's what I mean. What if he's not really dead yet?

Al kicks the corpse.

Al: Seems dead to me.

Angel: But how can you be sure? Maybe he's only brain dead. Or maybe his brain is fine but the rest of him is dead.

Al leans over. Touches the man's hands.

Al: He feels warm.

Excited now he looks for a pulse in the man's neck.

He's got a pulse! It's weak but it's a pulse. I better rob him before he dies.

Al grabs the tin. He pulls. But the man's fingers are frozen around it in a vise-like grip. Al pulls harder. He drags the man across the stage but without extracting the tin from his hands.

Isn't it disgusting. Even as they're dying they clutch at consumer goods.

Al pulls again. Angry. But no success.

Angel: Need some help?

Al: No, I can handle it.

Stops pulling. Ponders what to do. Has an idea. Sits down in front of the man. Puts his feet on the man's shoulders for support, grabs the tin and pulls back as if rowing. Pulls hard. Grunts. Groans. His feet slip off the man's shoulders and the momentum of the pull causes him to fall back pulling the man on top of him. At that moment the man comes to life, a horrible life at that. He screams and letting go of the tin whips out a knife intent on plunging it into Al's heart. Al is screaming. The man is screaming himself. Angel watches. Al is holding back the hand with the knife. He's desperate.

Al: HELP. HELP.

Angel: I asked you if you needed help and you said, No. You said you could handle it. Were you wrong?

Al: HELP.

Angel: Were you wrong?

Al: Alright! I was wrong!

Angel comes over behind the man. Grabs his head by the chin and gives his head a swift terrible twist, breaking his neck. The man collapses.

Angel: I think he's dead now.

Al crawls out from under the body with the tin in his hands.

Al: But we robbed him while he was still alive and therefore, scruplewise, I'm in the clear. It's tea-time!

He starts opening the tin. Angel crowds in. Al turns away from him and opens it. He laughs. Hands the tin over to Angel.

Here, eat.

Angel looks inside the tin.

Angel: SNAPSHOTS!

Rummages through the snapshots.

All this for some snapshots!

Al comes and looks over his shoulder at the pictures.

Al: Don't they look happy. Look at that. Crystal glasses raised high in a toast to something. Ah, the good old days.

Angel: I'm hungry. I'm tired of being hungry.

Al: Get thirsty then. C'mon.

Grabs the tin from his hands. Puts the lid back on it. Tosses it next to the dead man. Gestures to Angel toward the cart.

Moving on.

Angel: I need some food.

Al: Forget food. C'mon. Forget all about it. You eat it and it just turns to shit anyway. So let us instead address ourselves to the eternal and imperishable music of the ages. I said I would quiz you later. This is later.

Angel starts pulling the cart.

Al: We will now review our survey of classical music.

Are you ready?

Angel: I guess I'm as ready as I'll ever be, Al.

Al stops. Angel stops. Al looks at him.

Al: I'm not Al. While class is in session, I'm Mentor. I'm your Mentor. If you wish to address me, you may address me as Mentor. When class is not in session, I'm Al. How many times do we have to go through this?

Angel: Sorry.

Al: Fine. Are you ready?

Angel: I'm ready, Mentor.

Al turns around and starts walking. Angel pulls the cart and follows. Al vocalizes the grail motif.

Angel: The grail motif from *Parsifal*, by Richard Wagner. 1813-1883. Right?

Al: Right.

He vocalizes another selection.

Angel: The *Nocturne in E Flat, Opus 9, Numero 2* by Frederick Chopin. 1810-1849. Right?

Al: Right.

He vocalizes yet another selection.

Angel: I got it! I got it! The Sonata Number 12 in F,

Kerschel listing numero 332, by Johannes Chrysostomus Wolfgangus Amadeus Mozart. 1756-1791. Right?

Al: Right.

Angel: Alright.

He stops suddenly. We hear the buzzing of flies.

Wait a minute, Al.

Both are frozen, looking out and down at something.

You see that soccer stadium down there?

Al: Looks like a mass grave. They don't even bury them anymore. The smell!

Angel: That's where the big concert was held. Right there. That's where I heard Jesus Christ. The place was packed.

Al: It's still packed.

Angel: With corpses.

Al: So what? C'mon. Let's have a little Beethoven.

Al vocalizes from 'Ode to Joy' Angel follows, pulling the cart, looking back over his shoulder.

They exit.

SCENE FOUR

Interior of a bombed-out church. Day. Fragments of shattered stained glass windows still remain in place. It's raining. Thunder and lightning. The cart off to the side. Al is tinkering with a damaged church piano. Trying to fix it. Plinking the keys and then checking the interior, etc. He's a lover of musical instruments, not just music. Angel walks around slowly. Looks at Al. Al is totally preoccupied with his work. Angel, lonely, walks away. Stops. Looks about the place.

Angel: Do you think this was once a church?

Al: Of course it was, what do you think?

Angel: It's hard to tell. So many churches were converted to theatres that you can't really be sure when you see the ruins of a church that it really was a church. Maybe it was a theatre.

Al: Churches are theatres.

Angel: A lot of them are now, that's what I'm saying.

Al: No, that's not what you're saying. You're saying that a lot of the theatres were once churches and were then converted to theaters.

Angel: A lot of them were, weren't they?

Al: Never mind.

Lights a cigarette butt. Continues tinkering with the piano.

Angel: What's that instrument called that looks like a big violin?

Al: A bass. A cello.

Angel: A cello. That's what it was. That's what Jesus was playing. A cello.

Al: Do you remember the piece He played?

Angel: He didn't say what it was called. He just started playing.

Al: How did it go?

Angel: Alright, I guess. Who am I to criticize?

Al: No. No. The melody. The theme. Do you remember how it went?

Angel: No.

Al: But you were there?

Angel: Sure I was there, but by the time I got there, this soccer stadium was filled. Jammed. People down on the grass. Up on the bleachers. I was so far back and up so high, I could barely see Him.

Al: But you did see Him?

Angel: I saw Him alright. Although now it feels like I didn't. I mean, I know I did, but I don't feel like I did.

Al: He didn't preach? No sermons? He just played?

Angel: He just played. I've never listened so hard in my life. I was really trying. This is Jesus Christ, I kept thinking. This is it. The Second Coming. But I don't know. It didn't really . . . He was so far away and all . . . it wasn't what I thought it'd be.

Al: Why did you go in the first place?

Angel: I had this idea that maybe He would see something in me.

Al: See what?

Angel: Something. I mean when you come right down to it, I can't see shit in myself but I figured that maybe I wasn't objective. So I thought that maybe Him being Jesus, Son of God and all, maybe He'd look at me and go: Whoa! You there. Yes, you, stranger. I see something very significant in you.

Al: You didn't really think that, did you?

Angel: I did.

Al: So what happened?

Angel: I told you. I was up so high and so far back . . . I don't know.

Al: Well, He's dead now.

Angel: I thought He was put in prison by some faction. You know, like a hostage.

Al: I heard they killed Him.

Angel: It was going to be such a big thing, I thought. The Second Coming. I was sure something significant would happen.

Al: It did. Half a dozen new religious factions came into being and the Civil War really took off.

Angel: To me! I thought something significant would happen to me!

Al: I guess it didn't.

Angel: No, it didn't. I mean, there I was. Thousands of people. Thousands! And Jesus Christ, Son of God playing. And I was as lonely as ever. Can you beat that, Al! What's with me, anyway? What, I've got some genetic defect or something. Some extra lonely chromosome I inherited from my parents whoever the fuck they were. I was found on a doorstep of a church like this, or maybe it was a theatre. It just goes on, this feeling. . .

Al: Alright. Alright. I get it already. You are lonely.

Al starts plinking on the piano, playing some classical phrase, humming along to himself. The musical interruption hits Angel all wrong. Each note that Al plays is like a lash. He's simmering, trying not to be bothered, but something keeps on building and building and finally he explodes. Screams and flings himself upon Al. Throws him to the ground. Hits the piano keys with his fists. If he could, he would turn it over.

Angel: That's it! That does it! I've waited long enough and I'm not gonna wait anymore. Let's get down to it, Al.

Al backs away as he gets up.

Al: What?

Angel: I said, let's get down to it!

Al: Down to what?

Angel: I want some intimacy. I want some goddamn intimacy around here and I want it now. Right now.

Al: What's the matter with you?

Angel: I can't stand this anymore. I'm sick and tired of the fine arts, Al. Opus this, opus fucking that. I thought we'd be chums by now. At this rate, if something is not done soon, we'll never be chums. So I'm doing something about it. Here's the deal, Al. Either you open up or I'll kill you.

Al: You must be mad.

Angel: I want to get to know you, Al. Tell me something personal about yourself.

Al: I don't do that anymore.

Angel: Fine. I'll go first. I'll tell you something very personal about me.

Al: I don't want to hear it.

Angel: I'm lonely!

Al: So what?

Angel: Why should I be lonely if you're here?

Al: Why not?

Angel: If we were chums, I wouldn't be lonely. I have a right to know after all this time whose fucking cart I'm pulling, whose shit I'm taking, who it is I'm talking to. Who the fuck are you, Al?

Al: I'll tell you since you want to know. There's two of us here and since I'm not you, I must be somebody else. That's who I am. I'm somebody else.

Angel: I'M LONELY, AL! And it's up to you to do something about it.

He flings himself upon Al and starts choking him.

I WANT YOU TO KNOW ME!

He seems to be strangling him.

AND I WANT TO KNOW YOU!

Al, caught in the iron grip of Angel's hands, is desperately fishing around inside his clothes with one hand and with the other, pushing back Angel's face. A knife appears in his hand. He slashes Angel with it. Angel lets him go. They stand there, confronting each other. Angel is wiping the blood of his wound. Al is rubbing his throat, trying to get back his breath. He holds out the knife, but Angel, despite the knife, seems ready to attack again.

Angel: That knife don't scare me. I don't mind bleeding.

He advances slowly. Al, warding him off with the knife, backs off.

See. If I killed you, then at least I'd know why I'm lonely. Cause I'd be here all by myself.

Al: You want to be a free man? Do you? We're almost

there. But you have to pull the cart.

Angel: Pull this, professor.

Grabs his crotch.

I'm not going to be your ox anymore.

Al: Whose ox do you want to be?

Angel: I'm a human being!

Al: So?

Angel: So if you can't love me, you sonovabitch, the least you can do is treat me with dignity.

Al: How convenient. When he wants dignity: He's a human being. Then when he gets bored and kills just for kicks, he says: Hey, what can I do. I'm only human, after all. Human nature covers everything. I'm sick of it. It means nothing anymore to be human.

It's stopped raining. We better get going.

Al's reasoning befuddles Angel and although he can't find an eloquent counter-argument, he goes on hurting, and needing to express it.

Angel: I don't think you understand me, Al. This . . . this lonely hurting. I just have a need to share it with . .

Al: No. Not with me, you don't. I'm trying to get away from all this sharing we're having. What the hell do you think Civil War is but an orgy of sharing.

Angel: But, Al. You and I must have something in common, and I'm just . . .

Al: I have hardly anything left in common with myself. What could I possibly have in common with you? If you want to share something with me you must first elevate yourself a bit.

Angel grabs his crotch.

Angel: Elevate this.

Al: Look. Either pull the cart or get lost and I'll pull it myself.

Angel: I'm not pulling this fucking thing anymore!

Kicks the cart. But something about his bluster lacks conviction and Al is quick to see it.

Al: Fine. Then push it. As long as you keep up.

Angel grabs his crotch.

Angel: Keep this up, Professor.

He kicks the cart a couple of more times but he resumes his former position as the ox.

You highbrow motherfuckers are all alike, aren't you? You've never loved a living thing in your life, none of you.

Al: You do me wrong, scum. Millions. I've loved millions. The beauty of love is that it takes so little time. You can love a man, a woman, or all of mankind in less than five minutes, and then have the rest of the day to do the things you really like to do. Shall we?

Al leads. Angel, cursing under his breath, follows. They Exit.

SCENE FIVE

Night. A ravine. A fire is burning inside an oil drum. Full moon. The cart is upstage. The tarp is off. The statue is in the cart. All the paintings from the cart are downstage, arranged in a semi-circle and facing out. They're propped against rocks and other discarded rubbish in the ravine. Angel and Al are polishing the frames of the paintings.

Angel: I can't believe it. It's too good to be true. But it is true, isn't it, Al?

Al: Yes, it's true.

Angel: Show it to me again.

Al: Oh, c'mon.

Angel: Please.

Al: Alright.

He unfolds a map. Angel rushes over and looks down at it.

We're right here.

He points to the map.

And this over here is the border . . .

Angel: To the Land of the Free, right?

Al: Right.

Angel: We'll be there tomorrow, right?

Al: Right.

Angel: I've heard, I mean this is only what I've heard, but I've heard that the air itself in the Land of the Free, the very air you breathe is somehow . . .

He inhales with relish the imagined freedom.

Al: Yes, I've heard that too.

Angel: And I won't be lonely when we get there?

Al: No. Freedom is Father, from what I've heard. Freedom is Mother.

Angel: I've never had a Mom and Dad.

Al: You'll have both when we cross the border. Freedom is Sister. Freedom is Brother. The Friend you never had. Freedom's the Wife you love and the Children she bears you.

Angel: Sounds like Paradise.

Al: Yes.

He folds up the map. Angel goes back to polishing the frames.

Al: Careful! Don't touch the canvas. Only the frames. If we're lucky, it will be a sunny day tomorrow and the border guards will see us coming from their towers. They'll see the gilt-edged frames sparkling in the sunlight. The marble statue. The canvases. That way they'll know right away we're not just some miserable refugees fleeing for our lives. They have binoculars and it's important to create a good impression from a distance. Their border guards aren't just a bunch of goons, you know. They're the elite of their armed forces. Think of them as armed connoisseurs.

He gestures toward the paintings.

Which of these is your favorite?

Angel looks around.

Angel: I don't have one.

Al: You should.

Angel: Why's that?

Al: You just should. Just in case somebody asks you.

Angel: Who's gonna ask me?

Al: Never can tell. The border guards might.

Angel: I see. You better pick one out for me, Mentor.

looks at the canvases.

Al: How about that Goya over there?

Angel: Fine with me. Francisco José de Goya y Lucientes. 1746-1828. Right?

Al: Right.

Angel: You know what?

Al: What?

Angel: Feels pretty good having a favorite painter.

Al: It's just the beginning.

Angel: Oh, yeah?

Al: Sure. Once you become a free man you'll be free to have your very own favorite writer. A favorite philosopher. A favorite historian. A favorite period of history, a favorite string quartet, religion, restaurant. A complete cultural identity, that's what you'll have.

Angel: Oh, yeah?

Al: Sure.

Angel: A complete cultural identity?

Al: With all the trimmings.

Al stops polishing and so does Angel. Al picks up one of the paintings and takes it to the cart. Angel watches him.

Angel: How tenderly you do that, Al. I've only seen mothers carry their babes like that.

Al picks up another painting in the same way. Angel looks at him.

You must really love these things.

Al: Yes, I do.

Al will continue loading the cart until all the paintings are carefully put away during the remainder of this scene. Angel will help him.

Angel: Why do you love them so much?

Al: Because they speak to me.

Angel: But when I speak to you don't I speak to you?

Al: No.

Angel: So that's probably why you can't love me, right?

Al: Right.

Angel: Nobody's ever loved me that I'm aware of.

Al: Why should they?

Angel: I wasn't complaining. Just stating a fact. And nobody's ever seen anything in me.

Al: What's there to see in you?

Angel: Damned if I know. Tell me something.

Al: Yes?

Angel: If some great painter painted a portrait of me, would you love me a little then?

Al: I might love the portrait.

Angel: But not me?

Al: Of course not.

Angel: Why not?

Al: What did you have to do with it?

Angel: I'm in the fucking portrait, aren't I?

Al: No, you're not. The vision of the artist is in the portrait. You, me, today we're this, tomorrow we're that. We fumble around in confusion until we die. At best, man is chaos with a conscience. At worst, he's just chaos. Art never is. Art is freedom. When we're lost in the night, Art defines the darkness we're in, it elevates us to a promontory from where we can see the way. Forward and back. So we can discern the continuous or the severed line of our lives. And if we truly want to be human, it defines what that is and how far we have to go to reach it or how far off course we've strayed.

Angel: But what do you do if you can't live up to what you see?

Al: You suffer.

Angel: Wouldn't it be better not to suffer?

Al: Yes. I would prefer not to.

Angel laughs his scum-of-the-earth laugh.

What's so funny?

Angel: No offense, Al. But it's hard to imagine a guy like you suffering.

Al: Really? Alright. Shall we?

Al leads. Angel, now having second thoughts about having laughed, follows. They Exit.

SCENE SIX

High noon. From stage left to stage right and from downstage to upstage, railroad tracks fill the stage. They run in parallel and diagonal lines. Some are rusted. Grass is growing between them. Dead bodies here and there. Enter Al upstage right. He is hot and tired. He stops. Looks back. Waits a bit and starts moving again. He is followed by Angel, pulling the cart. Angel is exhausted. He's struggling to pull the wheels of the cart over the tracks. Grunts and strains and pulls. Gets them over one set of tracks and stops. Sits down.

Al: Don't stop. Whatever you do, don't stop now.

Angel: I've had it. I gotta rest.

Al: We're almost there. Look!

Points out toward the audience.

That's the border.

Angel looks.

Angel: What's the border?

Al: See that flag?

Angel: What flag?

Al: See that little thing that's fluttering up there, way up there way up there in the distance? See the stars?

Angel: Everything's fluttering. We went too fast. The pace was too fast.

Angel struggles to his feet again.

Al: Thatta boy.

Angel: What was that? Listen.

Both listen.

Al: It's nothing. It's somebody screaming, that's all.

Angel: It's somebody screaming?

Al: That's what I said. That's all it is. C'mon.

Angel looks around for the cause of the screaming.

Angel: Al. Look. There's someone moving in that pile of bodies.

Points off-stage. Al looks.

Al: So what. C'mon.

Angel is torn by what he sees. Wants to move forward. Starts. But stops again and looks in that direction. Releases the cart and heads in that direction. Al grabs him and holds him in place. He tries desperately to hold him back, but Angel is too strong and, in his plodding way, drags Al along. Suddenly a loud locomotive whistle is heard. Both freeze instantly. They look at each other. Then they look around. The sound of an approaching train is heard, but it's hard to tell from what direction it's coming. They look around in all directions.

Angel: I thought the trains weren't running anymore. I thought they were all bombed and destroyed.

Al: So did I.

Another loud locomotive whistle, louder and closer than before. They stand there, frozen and terrified, not knowing where to go or what to do. Angel once again looks offstage toward the cry he had heard and suddenly we see that he has made a decision. Starts to go in that direction. Al tries to hold him back. The two of them are struggling and screaming at each other, but we can't hear them over the sound of the approaching train. Angel breaks free and runs offstage. Al, alone and terrified, doesn't know what to do. Starts to run downstage toward the border. Stops. Realizes the cart is behind him. Runs back to the cart. Tries to pull it with fanatical desperation. Just as he manages to budge it forward, the speeding train is upon him. He turns. Looks. Sees it coming and we go to Black. In the darkness, the sound of the train continues. The train has blocked our view of Al.

Maybe we catch brief glimpses of him between the railroad cars as the train goes by. Maybe we even have flash images of the windows of the railroad cars. Maybe even images of the passengers looking out of the windows. And then the train goes by and we're back to light again. Al stands where he stood, next to the cart, the sound of the train fading away. Enter Angel. He's carrying a limp body of a Little Girl in his arms. He looks both bewildered and apologetic that he's doing what he's doing. Al turns and sees him. Shakes his head in disgust. Tries to keep his anger in check.

Angel: The train was gonna run her over. I got there in the nick of time. I saved her life, Al.

Al: That's nice. That's wonderful. You must feel so good inside now. Are you ready?

Angel: I think I am. Yes. Here we go.

He starts to put the Little Girl on top of the tarp on the cart, but Al instantly stops him.

Al: Oh, no, you don't. She stays behind.

Angel: But, Al. Her legs are broken. She can't walk. I think she's been raped over and over again. She was covered with semen. Her face, her legs, her . . .

Al: I get it. I get it.

Angel: I had to biff her one and knock her out. She

thought I was one of those others come back to mess with her some more.

Al: We have no time to argue. She's not going on my cart. Drop her and let's go.

Angel: But, Al. Look at her.

Al: I've looked at her already. I get it.

Angel: I can't just drop her now.

Al: Look, blockhead. The trains are running again. And that means that maybe one of those factions has won the war. And that means somebody'll be in charge soon and if we don't get the hell out of here and across the border, the borders will be closed and we'll be stuck here forever. So drop her and let's get going while there's still time.

Angel: But I saved her life.

Al: Right. You saved her life. You've done your part. Now drop her and let's go.

He tries to pull her out of Angel's arms. Angel swings her away, out of his reach.

Angel: But then it was all for nothing. What'd I save her life for if I'm just gonna drop her now?

Al: So you can learn an important lesson, you scum.

Saved her life! Does she look saved? You think that's all it takes. One shot salvation. There, I've done it. Now on to the next one. Do you have any idea the kind of love it takes to save somebody? Especially these little ones. She'll need to be saved every hour of every day over and over again for years and years. Are you willing to do that? Are you?

Angel: I don't know. I don't think so.

Al: Then drop her before she opens her eyes and starts hoping. DROP HER!

His shouting brings the Little Girl to life. She starts to scream in some foreign language: Persian, Arabic, maybe. As she's screaming, she's wrapping her arms around Angel's neck, clinging to him, pleading in her own language to Angel to save her, to be good to her, not to abandon her. Angel is totally confused. Al's warning has its effects.

Angel: What's she saying?

Al: What do you think she's saying? She needs to be saved again. You just saved her and already she needs to be saved again. Drop her! Let her go.

Angel: Alright. ALRIGHT!

He screams out like a man who has defeated some inner opponent. He tries to rid himself of the little girl, but she clings to him in desperation.

Screaming herself, pleading, clinging. Angel is now acting like a man who's being attacked by the victim he had saved. He's screaming and trying to pry her loose as if she were a human leech. He finally pulls her off. Hits her. Knocks her out. Dumps her aside, on top of another corpse. Grabs the cart and, both exhausted and frantic, begins to pull. They're both on a treadmill now. Running toward the audience, toward the flag, toward the border, toward freedom. There is no end to railroad tracks. They may move past them as they move forward, but new ones come. They keep running. Angel stumbles and falls. Al stops. Goes back. Rips the tarp off. Grabs a painting out of the cart. Helps Angel up to his feet. Looks out.

Al: They're looking at us. I caught a glint of light. They've got their binoculars trained on us. We gotta look good for them. We gotta let them know we're not just some refugee trash. C'mon.

And again they run on the treadmill toward freedom. Al is showing off his painting as he runs, hoping the Guards see it. Both are shouting.

Al: Please. Don't shoot!

Angel: Don't shoot!

Al: We're bringing culture. We are worthy! We are worthy!

Angel: Mozart! Rembrandt! Goya! Beethoven! We are worthy! We are worthy!

And as they run, both of them break into a duet, vocalizing 'Ode to Joy', performing, hoping to please. They run on, singing, when suddenly we hear a loud, strange sound. Like a long steel door rolling shut. And then the thunder of it shutting. They stop in their tracks. We hear the synchronized sound of marching boots. Coming toward them.

Angel: What do we do now?

Al: You let me do all the talking, alright?

Angel: Alright, Mentor.

Al: Call me Al.

Angel just nods. They stand there and raise their arms in the air. The sound of marching boots comes closer and closer.

Blackout.

END OF ACT I

ACT TWO

SCENE ONE

Just before dawn. Angel and Al are both standing on high stools. Their legs are tied around the ankles. Their hands are tied behind their backs. Both have nooses around their necks. The taut ropes are tied to something high over their heads. They're both standing there, looking out. Then Angel turns his head and looks at Al. Al feels his stare, but does not acknowledge it. Angel makes a sarcastic grunt. Al sighs, looking away now.

Angel: So. Here we are, huh? You let me do all the talking. Isn't that what you said? I mean, correct me if I'm wrong, but wasn't that what you said and didn't you say it in that way of yours, like you were on top of the situation, so on top of it and all? You let me do all the talking, I believe was what you said.

Al: Alright. I said it.

Angel: Good thing, huh? I mean good thing I didn't do all the talking. I'd hate to think what might've happened to us had I done all the talking. We might be in a real jam now, had I done all the talking.

Al: I did the best I could.

Angel: This. This is the best you could do. You're one crafty negotiator, Mentor.

Al: It was too late for negotiations. Had you not wasted all that time with the little girl, we could have been across the border now.

A beat.

I wish I had a favorite philosopher. I could sure use one now.

Al: What about Schopenhauer?

Angel: Arthur Schopenhauer. 1788-1860.

Al: Right. What about him?

Angel: What about him?

Al: That's what I'm asking you: What about him?

Angel: Oh. No. I don't think he's for me. From what you've told me about him, he's a bit too pessimistic for my taste.

A beat of silence.

Apropos of nothing?

Al: Yes?

Angel: Why are they hanging us?

Al: It's a cornerstone of the new government's judicial system: Hang them—they'll know why. They provide the gallows. It's up to us to provide the guilt.

Angel: For once I did something right.

Al: Meaning what?

Angel: I had a feeling it would come to this. You know. What lay in store for me. That's why I've lead a life of crime. So I could be guilty of something. Just in case. I'm way ahead of the game now. I can think of a dozen reasons why I deserve to be hung.

Al: So can I.

Angel: When are they gonna hang us?

Al: Sunrise.

Angel: You don't know what time it is now, do you?

Al: A bit before death, I think.

A beat of silence.

Angel: The worst day of my life was the day I met you.

Al: That's a fine thing to say to somebody who rescued you.

Angel: The way I see it, I had a noose around my neck when we met and I've got a noose around my neck now. You didn't rescue me. All you did was prolong my hanging. I could've been nice and dead by now instead of standing here, all tense and terrified.

Al: But what about all that extra life you got to live, thanks to me.

Angel: What about it?

Al: What do you mean: What about it?

Angel: That's what I mean: What about it?

Al: Had you died before we met, you would have died stupid. Think of all the things you've learned from me. Music. History. Philosophy. Art. Your vocabulary has improved. Think of all the progress you have made.

Angel: If progress leads to getting hung, I don't get it. What's the point of progress if I'm gonna die?

Al: There! You see what I mean?

Angel: See what?

Al: The question you just posed. Do you realize that

you have just asked the central question of man's whole existence?

Angel: Good for me.

Al: What's the point of progress if we're all going to die?

Angel: Didn't I just say that?

Al: That's what I'm telling you. When we met, you would have been incapable of understanding such a question, to say nothing of being able to pose it yourself. See what I mean?

Angel: No.

Al: Thanks to me, you have made enormous strides, made remarkable progress.

Angel: WHAT PROGRESS?

Al: Mankind has been asking itself that question for eons. Some of the greatest thinkers, prophets, philosophers, have asked themselves that very question. What, in fact, is the point of progress if, in fact, we are all going to die?

Angel: I've just asked the same question that mankind's been asking itself for eons and you tell me that's progress?

Al: Enormous progress for you. For the rest of mankind that's already been asking itself that question, it's the same old story.

Angel: So what's the answer?

Al: To what?

Angel: To the question of the eons.

Al: There is no answer.

Angel: There is no answer?

Al: No.

Angel: So mankind's been asking itself the same old question for eons, to which there is no answer and progress is getting as many people as possible to ask the question.

Al: Now you've got it.

Angel: Oh, shit!

Al: What?

Angel: Here comes the sun.

Al: Let us try and appreciate the irony: Lights out at sunrise.

Angel: I don't wanna die!

A ray of the rising sun hits their faces. A military-style bugle blows off-stage. Angel listens to it. Thinks. Responds.

Bizet. George Bizet. 1838-1875. Right?

Al: Right.

The bugle stops. They wait in silence as more sunlight hits them.

Enter a Hangman. Dressed in black with a black hood over his head so that only his eyes and mouth show. He comes toward them. Inspects one and then the other with a discerning air. Then he goes toward Al.

Hangman: We might have a business proposition for you.

Al: I'll do anything. Absolutely anything.

The Hangman takes the noose off his neck.

Hangman: We're not making any promises. It all depends on the interview.

Starts leading him away.

If you're not used to interviews here's a helpful hint. Just be yourself.

Angel stands there with a noose around his neck

watching them leaving.

Angel: Al?

Al and the Hangman exit. Angel remains. Looks out. Blackout.

SCENE TWO

Same as before. Angel is on the stool, with the noose around his neck. Looking around. Enter Al, pulling the cart, but the cart is empty.

Angel: Al. What's going on?

Al comes over to him. Takes out a knife. Cuts his legs free. Then cuts his hands. Angel is suspicious and hesitant, but he does remove the noose from his neck.

Is this deja-vu or what?

Al: Maybe now you won't think I'm such a bad negotiator.

Angel: I don't know what to think, Al. I'm afraid to think. I mean, I thought I was gonna die. I'd hate to think I'm not, if I still am. I mean, am I free?

Al: We're both free. With conditions.

Angel: Real free?

Al: Real free with real conditions.

Angel: I don't mind any conditions as long as I'm free.

Al: Then you're free.

Angel: What are the conditions?

Al: I got us a job.

Angel: A job?

Al: That's right.

Angel: What kind of job?

Al: It's only a part-time job.

Angel: So is life, it seems.

Al: My point exactly.

Angel: Meaning what?

Al: The two go hand in hand. Quid pro quo, if you know what I mean.

Angel: I'm not sure I do.

Al: No job: No life.

Angel: Is that how it was put to you?

Al: In so many words.

Angel: We accept this job, we live. We don't accept, we die?

Al: Exactly.

Angel: What's the job?

Al: It's a part-time job.

Angel: I already know that part. What's the other part?

Al: What other part?

Angel: The 'do' part. What do we have to do?

Al: Render a service.

Angel: It's a service industry we're working for?

Al: In a manner of speaking, yes. Public service.

Angel: The government, we're working for the government?

Al: Part-time.

Angel: I didn't know there was a government.

Al: There is now.

Angel: Then the Civil War is over.

Al: For the time being.

Angel: Who won?

Al: The government we're working for. It's a coalition, I think, of all the former implacable foes. A brand new flag was waving outside the ministry of the interior.

Angel: What do we have to do?

Al: Kill a man.

Angel: One man?

Al: Just one.

Angel: What man?

Al: Part-time man.

Angel: Part-time man?

Al: Yes. Part-time man. Part-time Messiah.

Angel: Jesus?

Al: Yes.

Angel: Jesus Christ?

Al: Yes, Jesus Christ.

Angel: We have to kill Jesus Christ!

Al: We don't have to.

Angel: To live, I mean.

Al: Yes. If we want to live, we have to kill Him.

Angel: I thought they already killed Him.

Al: So did I. But they didn't. They took Him prisoner and took Him to this place outside the city.

He takes out a map. Unfolds it.

Here. They gave me a map. How to get there. It's right here, see?

He points to a spot on the map. Angel looks.

Angel: I don't get it.

Al: What now?

Angel: Why didn't they kill Him?

Al: They who?

Angel: They they. The government.

Al: The government is a concept. Concepts can't do anything. The government doesn't kill people. People kill people.

Angel: Why do we have to kill him? I mean, I know why. To save our ass. But why did they choose us? Why didn't they choose somebody else?

Al: To them, we are somebody else.

Angel: But why not some other somebody else? Why us?

Al: What difference does it make? Had they chosen some other somebody else they'd be standing here just like we're doing and asking themselves the same question: Why did they choose us instead of somebody else? You can still choose death if you want.

Angel: What about you?

Al: After much agony, I've decided to choose death for Jesus Christ instead. Are you in or are you out?

Angel: I'm in, but I'd like a couple of minutes to agonize over it.

Al: Fine.

Angel: The way I see it, somebody's gonna kill Jesus, if not us, then somebody else, right?

Al: Right.

Angel: And who's to say who that other somebody else might be. For all we know he might be a family man. Whose wife loves him. Whose children adore him. Whose neighbors respect him. Knock! Knock! There's a knock on his door. Hello, you have been chosen to kill Jesus Christ. Somebody else was chosen, but he refused and because he refused you have been picked to do the job. Oh, Al! The poor guy! He can't win. If he refuses, they'll kill him and who'll feed his family. If he accepts he becomes a murderer. His kids don't adore him anymore. His wife leaves him. It's very tempting, Al, to worry about my own scruples at a time like this, but I just don't know if I can plunge that poor guy into the jaws of this dilemma.

Al: It would be pretty cruel of you if you did.

Angel: You're right. So the responsible thing to do, the humanitarian thing to do, the Christian thing to do is to kill Christ.

Al: Talk about brilliant agony. That was magnificent. Top drawer.

Angel: It made me feel so good I could agonize some more.

Al: Better save some for after we kill Him.

Angel: You're right.

Takes a look at the empty cart.

What happened to your art collection?

Al: It's been confiscated by the state. When we bring back the body of Christ, they promised to return it. Not only that, we get exit visas. We bring back the body, get our stuff and our visas and across the border we go.

Angel: To the Land of the Free, right?

Al: Right.

Angel: Alright.

Angel pulls the cart. Al leads. They Exit.

SCENE THREE

In the darkness, we hear Gregorian chants. Lights up. We're in a monastery. Center stage, there's a chair. Al and Angel are standing still. Waiting. Both are ill at ease. Both are smoking. The Gregorian chants continue. Enter a Monk. He is smiling his serene smile and continues to smile it off and on during this scene.

Monk: Welcome. Welcome. We've been expecting you. Forgive me, please, but this is consecrated ground . . . if you wouldn't mind . . .

Gestures to their cigarettes. They put them out.

Thank you. Thank you. We abstain from everything here. Almost. You are who I presume you to be, are you not? You have come from Caesar?

Al: Caesar?

Monk: Forgive the terminology. Tradition. We still refer to that outside world, the world outside these walls, as Caesar's. This is the world of the spirit. That is the world of the flesh. This one is ruled by the Holy Spirit. That one is ruled by Caesar.

Al: We've come from out there on orders of the new government, if that's what you mean.

Monk: That's exactly what I mean. Exactly. You have your orders, I suppose.

Al: Yes. We are here to render a service.

Monk: And we are here to render unto Caesar what is Caesar's. I will bring in the prisoner shortly, but before I do, is there anything we can do to make the task at hand easier to bear? A glass of port? It's from our own vineyards.

Al: No.

Monk: A slice of bread? Baked right here.

Al: No.

Angel: I wouldn't mind a sandwich myself.

Monk: Sorry. No sandwiches. But I can offer you absolution for what you're about to do.

Al: That's alright. We come pre-absolved.

Monk: Well, make yourself . . .

Gestures like a host.

I have to go back. We were in the middle of our midmorning prayers. But I'll return with the prisoner shortly. Make yourself . . .

Gestures. Smiles. Leaves. As soon as he's gone, Al and Angel light up again.

Al: Nervous?

Angel: No, it's nothing. Just nerves.

Angel listens and half hums along with the Gregorian chants he hears. He's very nervous.

Angel: Gregorian chant. Introduced under Pope Gregory I, 540-604 A.D. Right?

Al: Right.

Angel: And while we stand here waiting, we're waiting according to the Gregorian Calendar. Introduced by Gregory the 13th. Real name, Ugo Buoncompagni. 1502-1585.

Al: Right.

A beat or two as they wait.

Angel: Time doesn't exactly fly by under the Gregorian Calendar. How long we gotta wait?

Al: Until they stop chanting.

Angel: What's to stop them?

Al: Take it easy. We'll be out of here soon.

Angel: Out where?

Al: Out there. And from there, across the border and into:

Angel: The Land of the Free, right?

Al: Right.

Angel: And when I get there, I won't feel bad anymore about anything I've done up to now or anything I'm gonna have to do from now on 'til I get there, right?

Al: Right. You'll be free of everything you're not free of now.

Angel: I don't feel free of anything now. I feel totally trapped.

Al: So much the better. You'll be that much freer when you get there.

Angel: It's too bad I gotta commit a murder in the first degree just so I can be free.

Al: Freedom doesn't come cheap.

The Gregorian chant stops. The sudden silence affects both of them. Both get a little more nervous. They put out their cigarettes and light up new ones.

Enter Jesus, carrying a cello and a bow, followed by the Monk. Angel and Al quickly put out their cigarettes. Jesus has been tortured. He is bloodied and bleeding. Head bowed.

Monk: Here he is. I'll leave Him in your hands. The service you have to render should be rendered in what . . . five, ten minutes. I'll be back in a bit.

He leaves. Jesus remains standing upstage, near the

chair. Angel and Al are downstage, frozen in place. For beat or two, the three of them just stand there like three statues. Then, at the same time, Al and Angel turn away from Jesus and light up cigarettes. Both are very nervous.

Angel: He's been tortured.

Al: So what ?

Angel: I don't know. I didn't expect it, that's all.

Looks over his shoulder at Jesus.

He looks real bad. Why don't we just let Him die of His wounds?

Al: Because if we don't kill Him, the deal's off and they'll kill us.

Angel: But to kill somebody who's been tortured already . . .

Al: The way I see it, it would be morally wrong to just stand here and let Him suffer. If we kill Him, we'll be doing the moral thing, alleviating his miseries.

Angel: But to do the moral thing, we have to commit murder.

Al: Yes. But a moral murder. So, c'mon. Get it over with.

Angel: Wait a minute. You mean I gotta do it?

Al: Who else?

Angel: There's two of us here. Why not you?

Al: Because killing seems more in line with your character than mine.

Angel: Not anymore. Thanks to you, Mentor, I've made enormous progress. Think of all the things I've learned from you. Music. History. Philosophy. Art. My vocabulary has improved. I'm not the same man anymore because thanks to you, Mentor . . .

Al: Alright! We'll flip a coin.

He fishes a coin out of his pocket. Angel examines it. Looks at both sides, to make sure it has two sides. Gives it back to Al.

Al: I'll flip it and you call it. Or do you want to flip it and I'll call it? Or I could both flip it and call it, unless you'd rather do both?

It's too many choices for Angel.

Angel: You decide.

Al: I'll flip it and you call it.

Al flips the coin in the air.

Angel: Heads.

The coin lands on the floor. Both look.

Angel nods. Al takes out his knife. Hands it to Angel Angel is horrified by the sight of it. Doesn't want to take it. While he hesitates, Jesus sits down. Angel finally takes the knife. Knife in hand, but very hesitant, he turns and heads toward Jesus. Jesus begins to play . Angel stops in his tracks as soon as he hears the music.

Al: What're you waiting for?

Angel: I don't know. It's this music. Listen.

Al: I don't have to listen. It's not like He's playing something new. I've heard this piece many times before. It's Bach. Don't you get it? That's all it is. It's Bach.

Angel: I think it's the same thing He played at that concert, the last time I saw Him.

Al: So what?

Angel: I don't know. At that time He was too far away. I could barely see Him. And now what? He's too close, is that it? Why doesn't something significant happen to me, Al?

Al: This is no time for personal problems. You want something significant to happen to you? Here's something. If you don't kill Him we're dead. Can't have anything more significant than that. Do you want to die?

Angel: Okay. Okay. I'll do it. But I gotta get in the right mood first.

Al: You're just standing there.

Angel: I am poised. Ready to strike.

Al: Then strike away.

Angel: I can't strike until I'm in the right mood to strike. You mind?

Al: You're backing out.

Angel: I'm not backing out of anything. Look. I said I'll do it and I'll do it. Isn't my word good enough?

Al: Your work isn't going to kill anyone.

Angel: What am I supposed to do? Just go up to Him and plunge this knife in His back?

Al: Nobody really cares how you do it.

Angel: But since I'm the one that has to do it, I care.

Looks at the knife.

What kind of knife is this, anyway?

Al: Will you just . . .

The Monk enters. Angel reacts to seeing him by getting tough with Jesus. Very threatening.

Angel: You're a dead man. You know that? You're dead. I mean, you are dead.

Al: My friend, the murderer, has to get in the mood to murder, it seems.

Monk: It's not going to take much longer, is it?

Angel: I don't know. I mean, it's bad enough I have to commit a mortal sin without at least being properly worked up when I do it.

Monk: What mortal sin, my son?

Angel: I'm not your son. To kill Him, that's what sin.

Monk: I've read the Bible from cover to cover countless times and there is no mention of that sin anywhere.

Angel: Oh, no? What about: Thou shalt not kill. What about that?

Monk: Man, man. Not God. The Bible makes no mention of the sin of killing God.

Angel turns to Al.

Angel: Al?

Al: Technically, he's correct.

Angel: I just don't understand. Why does He have to die?

Al: You know why. So we can save our ass.

Angel: I know that part. But why does everybody else want Him to die? What has He done?

Al: What does it matter? We made a deal and . . .

The Monk cuts Al off.

Monk: No, no. Please. It's a valid question.

To Angel.

Is that what's troubling you, my son?

Angel: I don't know what's troubling your son cause I'm not your son, but yes, that's what's troubling me.

Monk: He has to die so that we can move on with our lives. So that we can get on with our reforms. We want to overhaul our whole system and He's in the way.

Angel: What system?

Monk: *The* system. Life. Everything. We want to make moral integrity accessible to everyone. If you have a fixed standard, it's tough. But if you let all standards float, like currency, then everyone's got a shot. It will be a lot more democratic that way. Any other questions? Problems? Qualms?

Angel: No.

Monk: Good. In that case . . .

He gestures toward Jesus indicating that Angel should proceed with the killing. Angel heads toward Jesus. Looks very determined. Stops next to Him Raises knife as if about to strike and then suddenly tosses the knife on the ground.

Angel: I can't. I just can't kill somebody in His condition. You want me to kill somebody? Fine. Just don't torture him first. Look at Him. I wouldn't know where to stab Him without hitting a wound. Get Him some medical attention first. Let Him get well, rest up, recuperate. Then I'll kill Him.

Al: I knew it. I knew you'd let me down when it counted. After all I've done for you.

Angel: Look, man, you're down to one scruple. So am I. This is mine.

Al: You don't have any scruples. Why do you think I took you on in the first place?

Angel: I lied in my interview. I saw that the job you were offering called for somebody totally unscrupulous so I lied about my qualifications just to get the job. So fire me.

Al: We flipped a coin!

Angel: We didn't flip nothing. *You* flipped. And it was *your* coin.

Al: The fact remains we . . .

Monk intercedes.

Monk: Gentlemen. Gentlemen. Please. Let us not make a mockery of this moment. The Man, after all, is God.

A beat of silence. All three look at Jesus.

Angel: You're a fine one to talk. Here you are a high ranking member of some men on the cloth club and I bet you don't even believe in God.

Monk: Of course I believe.

Angel: How could you and still want to have Him killed?

Monk: I don't think you're capable of appreciating the finer points of my belief in God.

Al: He wouldn't know a fine point if you drove it up

his fingernails.

Monk: In the Idea of God. That's what I believe in. But I suspect you're friend can't discern the distinction between the two.

Al: You don't have to suspect. He couldn't discern his own mother if he saw her. But I certainly can, because I too believe in the Idea of God. In my opinion it is one of the greatest ideas of mankind.

Monk: If not the greatest.

Al: You took the "ipsissimi verba" out of my mouth. *The* greatest.

Monk: The "sine qua non" of the very idea of being a man.

Al: A "sui generis" idea which allows man to be "sui juris."

Monk: The Idea of God which *is* God belongs inside each one of us where we can continually refine and redefine its essence. But the problem, of course, is not the Idea. It's having a living, breathing God, not inside of us where He belongs but right there in front of our eyes. It makes for a cumbersome dilemma, if you know what I mean.

Al: I do indeed. How can we be free to interpret the

meaning and the nature of the eternal truth if that eternal truth becomes a man who says, in so many words, there is nothing to interpret anymore. Here I am.

Monk: Exactly. It's that very "Here I am, there is nothing to interpret anymore," that's unbearable.

Al: You want truth? Here it is. Here I am.

Monk: We never actually said that we wanted to find the truth. What we said was that we wanted to be free to pursue it.

Al: Pursue no more, He says. Here it is.

Monk: I know, I know. But we need to have something to pursue. Man, by his very nature, is a seeker.

Al: Seek no more, He says. It's all right here.

Monk: I know. I know.

Imagine, if you will, being an actor in a play, or for that matter, a member of the audience sitting in a theater and watching a play. It's a great play. An epic. A masterpiece. We are transported into the realm of Art itself. And then suddenly this long dead and half forgotten god of the theatre, some goddamned Euripides or Sophocles, drops down on the stage and refuses to leave. Doesn't say a word. Not a word. Just sits there. But without so much as saying a single word, his living, breathing presence reminds us what Art really is. One minute we were in a lofty epic of modern man, the next, thanks to him, we're in some cheap, banal melodrama we mistook for Art.

Al: Say no more. Kill him. Kill him.

Monk: Because if our show is to go on . . .

Al interrupts.

Al: It must. Our show must go on.

Monk: Then He must die.

Al: Even dying's too good for Him. I'd gladly do it myself. But I don't want to presume. So I'll flip you for the privilege of killing Him.

Al reaches inside his pocket. Takes out his coin.

Heads or tails?

The Monk, trapped by his own arguments, suddenly realizes what Al has done. But he seems to appreciate the talent it took. He smiles.

Al flips.

Monk: Heads.

The coin loin lands on the floor. Both look. It's hard

to tell by their reactions who won or who lost. Angel wants to have a look but Al puts his foot on the coin. The Monk walks away toward the knife. He picks it up. He seems to be heading back to Al to give it to him as he walks past Jesus when suddenly, without much malice, he turns and pulling back Jesus' head, he slits his throat. He drops the knife on the ground and exits. Neither Angel nor Al expected this to happen. Both are stunned as they approach the body of Jesus.

Angel: Is He dead?

Al feels for signs of life.

Al: Not yet.

They wait.

Now He is.

Angel: I can't think . . . my head is all . . . what do we do now?

Al takes a beat to think. Goes to the knife. Picks it up.

Al: Well . . . the way I see it . . . our orders were to bring back the body as proof of services rendered. Here's the weapon that was used.

Pockets the knife.

There's the body.

Angel's head is groggy. He's trying to hold it in one place and think.

Angel: You mean . . . we're going to tell them that we did it?

Al: Why not? This way we can fulfill our obligation and still be innocent of the crime. We get to have it both ways. What could be better? Let's get Him in the cart.

Angel lifts the body and puts it in the cart. Al puts in the cello and the bow. The monastery bell is ringing and now we hear the singing of Gregorian chants as Al leads and Angel pulls the cart and they exit.

SCENE FOUR

On the road. Day. Enter Al. Takes a few steps. Stops. Looks back over his shoulder. Lights a cigarette. Enter Angel, pulling the cart with the body of Jesus Christ and his cello inside. Seeing Angel coming Al starts to go. Seeing Al go Angel stops. Seeing Angel stop Al stops again.

Al: Something's the matter?

Angel: I'm tired.

He sits down, mind weary, soul weary and body weary. Al gives him his cigarette. Angel takes it. Takes a drag. Doesn't like something about it. Looks at it. Looks around.

Didn't we stop here once before?

Al: I don't know.

Angel: I think we did.

Al: Maybe. So what?

Angel: So here we are again.

Al: Pretty soon it'll be good-bye to all this. We hand over the body as proof of services rendered, we get our exit visas and our art collection and across the border we go . . .

Angel: To the Land of the Free, right?

Al: Right.

Angel: Everything is starting to feel like deja vu to me. We were here once before and here we are again going to the same place we were going the last time we stopped here on our way there.

Al: It's different this time.

Angel: We're not any different. We're exactly the same. Things happen but nothing really happens to us. We just go on.

Al: What do you want us to do?

Angel: I don't know.

Al: Are you going to smoke that cigarette or look at it?

Angel gives it back to Al.

Angel: Events don't even leave fingerprints on us. Nothing. We just go on.

Al: Like I said: What do you want us to do!

Angel: Like I said: I DON'T KNOW. I DON'T KNOW. But even a tree, even a fucking tree stump's got rings to show that it was alive and that things happened to it, whereas I, I've got nothing to show.

Al: What you have to show is this: You saved your own ass when others lost theirs. And when you come right down to it, that's what it's all about, isn't it?

Angel: I don't know. You tell me.

Al: That's what it's all about.

Angel: I'm getting sick and tired of saving my own ass.

Al: I know the feeling. But it won't last. You're just having a temporary crisis. Don't worry about it. It'll pass.

Angel: I *know* it'll pass. That's what's worrying me.

That's my crisis, Al. My crisis is that *all* my crises pass and when they do it's like nothing happened. I'm the same after the crisis as I was before. I resume. I move on. We just move on, Al. If this whole fucking world went up in flames and if we could, you and I would just move on up there through the galaxy, from planet to planet, watching other worlds going up in flames and even if the whole fucking creation was to go up in flames we'd still be exactly the same. What does it take, man? What the fuck does it take to . . .

Silence.

Al: I'm thinking.

Silence.

There was this child. A little girl. It could have been a little boy instead. A son. A daughter. What difference does if make: A loving child. But before her love could reach me I got it. There, I thought, that's love. I get it. And then I moved on. That's the problem.We get it.

Angel: Get what?

Al: You name it. People bleed before our eyes but in the midst of their agonies we get it. The problem is not that we're blind to their agonies or deaf to their cries, the problem is we get it and move on. Wars break out. We get it. Peace comes. We get it. Wars break out again. Once again we get it. We're always a step ahead of the game. There's only one god left. The I get it god.

And then suddenly the screaming sound of a low flying fighter jet squadron flies overhead. They follow it turning their backs to the audience. And we hear another sound. Low. Rumbling. The sound of a motorized division approaching. They turn around slowly to look at it, facing the audience.

Angel: There's a whole army coming this way.

Al: Tanks. Trucks. Helicopters. But look.

They watch in silence for a beat or two.

That flag. Look. It's the same flag we was at the border.

Angel: I see it. The stars! I see the stars.

Al: And it's coming toward us. We're being liberated. Don't shoot. Please don't shoot.

Angel: Don't shoot. Don't shoot.

Al: We're on your side. We killed Jesus Christ so that all men can be free. We're on your side. We are worthy.

Angel: We are worthy. We are worthy.

And then Al starts singing Beethoven's Ode to Joy. Angel feels the deja vu of it but joins in anyway. They're both singing when the choral arrangement of the song kicks in full blast as if in reply to their efforts. It's as if they hear it and respond, convinced as they sing on of a brotherly welcome. Blackout. The choral arrangement continues in the darkness.

SCENE FIVE

A mountaintop. There once was a forest here but years of war have devastated it leaving, if anything, a few charred tree trunks. Angel and Al are crucified. Al's head is hanging down. He's not moving. Angel is talking.

Angel: The first time I killed a man was in the ring. It was the last round and I was way behind on points so when I cought him with a solid right to the temple and saw that he was hurt I moved in for the kill. Pow. Pow. Pow. My only hope of winning was to knock him out. Pow. Pow. Pow. By now the guy's helpless. His arms are hanging down and he can't defend himself but the ref don't want to stop the fight. So I keep hitting him and hitting until he finally falls. The ref starts counting but at the sound of four the bell rings. The fight's over. He was dead. Not only was he dead but the doc at ringside pronounced him dead but get this . . . he still won the fight. On points. Saved by the bell. Can you beat that? So I thought to myself, hey, maybe I should consider getting out of this profession where you can lose to a dead man.

He's been looking at Al off and on while he talked and now he just looks at him. Silence. Al is not moving. Is he dead? Angel speaks to him, almost in a whisper.

Al?

With growing alarm.

Al!

With panic and grief.

AL!

Al, startled, lifts his head. Wide awake.

Al: What? What is it?

Angel: Nothing. I was just worried that . . . Nothing. Were you asleep?

Al: I don't know. Maybe.

Silence.

Angel: I'd hate to die in my sleep. I really would. You know. There you are sound asleep and then you're dead. You go from one darkness to another without even knowing you're going. On the other hand, I'd hate to wake up and then die. What did I wake up for? Just to die.

A beat.

I can't think of anything positive to say about death. Can you?

Al: Not off the top of my head, no.

Silence.

Angel: Apropos of absolutely nothing?

Al: Yes.

Angel: Why did they crucify us?

Al: As a lesson to others.

Angel: I know that much, but did they crucify us for killing Christ of for not killing Him and then lying and trying to take the credit for the murder?

Al: I don't think our liberators could decide themselves which was the worst offense so they crucified us under the catchall provision of crimes against humanity.

Angel: What kind of crimes would those be?

Al: Well, that gets tricky. See. Crimes against humanity are no different than acts committed in the name of humanity. It all depends on the time and the place and the status of humanity in question. Different times, different humanity.

Angel: I pity the poor bastards that come after us.

Al: What do you mean?

Angel: At this rate a person with an average intelligence won't have a chance. You'll have to be another Erasmus of Rotterdam if you want to know why you're being crucified.

A beat.

Speaking of which. Why did they have to work us over like that if they were going to crucify us anyway?

Al: Because we wouldn't cooperate.

Angel: Who in his right mind's gonna cooperate when being crucified?

Al: That's why they worked us over. To achieve cooperation. Were you rifle-butted or stabbed?

Angel: Stabbed. Kicked and stabbed but it was the stabbing that did the damage. I felt this bayonette go right through my stomach and hit the spine. And you?

Al: Rifle-butted. My ribs are broken. There's this ransacked feeling in my chest.

Angel: Ever since I can remember, anyone who ever knew me told me that someday I'd hang.

Both enjoy a small laugh.

Al: At least you proved them wrong.

Another small laugh is shared but out of it Angel sugues into a painful moan.

Angel?

Angel: A whole new kind of pain just said hello to me. I feel like I'm being separated like an egg yolk from the white. Oh, damn. It hurts. If I could just scream.

Al: I know. It would hurt tenfold if you did. All I have to do is raise my voice a little and my broken ribs plunge deeper into places where they don't belong.

Angel: What a thing. Crucified like dogs.

Al: Don't be silly. Who ever heard of dogs being crucified?

Al coughs but coughing hurts so he has to stifle it.

Angel: The thing I dread most about dying . . . Excuse me. Are you interested in this gibberish?

Al: Why not?

Angel: It's the dread of the grand deja vu just before I die. You know. Having my whole life flash before my eyes. What the hell is the point of having my whole life flash before my eyes when my life's been flashing before my eyes my whole life as it is? It keeps coming up, the same life, like a bad lunch I've had. The least you should get, seems to me, as compensation for dying, is to have somebody else's life flash before your eyes for once, so that, if nothing else, you get a little perspective as you're dying. It is your last chance, after all.

Al looks at him. Keeps on looking at him. Angel, troubled by the stare, grows uneasy.

Why are you looking at me like that?

Al: I've never said this to anyone in my life before. I've never even thought it of anyone or anything before now. I don't get you. I really don't get you. I don't get you at all.

Angel is defensive about this.

Angel: Can't blame me for that. I've tried to . . . you know . . . to open up and all. Doesn't matter. It's too late now.

Al: I have made a mousetrap out of my mind. The trap has been tripping and snapping the spines of moments that could have lived on in my life but I got them. And they died. There was nothing I didn't get. The gist of this. The gist of that. The gist of everything. The Torah, the Koran, the Bible, the Mahabaratha. I have read them in the original Hebrew, Arabic, Greek, Sanskrit, and got them, I have gotten the gist of them all. All I'm saying is this. Somehow, despite my efforts, I don't get you and I am so glad. So very, very, glad for both of us. That's all I meant.

Angel takes a beat. Having misunderstood him initially, he now has to consider what he has just heard.

We hear the sound of a small bell ringing. The

sound is coming closer. They both look around as best as they can. And then they both see something at the same time and continue looking in that direction from where: Enter a Young Boy. In one hand he has a small bell and in the other a long thin cane. The way he uses the cane tells us that he's blind. There is a rope around his waist and holding onto the end of the rope is our Monk. He is wearing dark glasses and he too is blind. Angel and Al look at them as they make their way. The Boy is feeling around with his stick for something he can't find. Stops. The Monk walks up to his back. Puts his hands on the Boy's shoulder.

Monk: Is something wrong?

Boy: I can't find any of the old landmarks that should be here. There should be an artesian well right here but I can't find it.

Listens.

And I hear no water running.

Smells the air.

There was supposed to be a beautiful forest here, but I can't detect the scent of trees and although I can feel a breeze in my face I hear no rustling of leaves overhead. Maybe we're not where we're supposed to be at all. Maybe I've led us astray, Sir. It's been a long time and maybe my memory played me false.

Monk: The wars have rearranged the way the cities look. Perhaps they've rearranged everything else as well.

Boy: In that case we're lost, Sir. All I have to go on is the landmarks that used to be here.

Monk: I wouldn't mind stopping and resting for a while.

They sit down. Al and Angel just look down at them. The Monk's feet hurt. He rubs them

I wonder if it's night or day. I don't know what difference it makes anymore. Idle curiosity.

Boy: Oh, there's no need to wonder, Sir. That much I know for sure. It's day. Can't you feel the sun? It's day alright. A sunny day.

The Monk puts his hand out trying to feel the sun.

Monk: No, I can't seem to feel it.

Boy: Feel the top of my head. Feel how warm it is.

The Monk does. Smiles.

Monk: Yes, you're right.

He leaves his hand on the top of the Boy's head, stroking it gently but very tentatively. The Boy smiles.

Boy: My father had this little joke he told whenever

we walked through here, if indeed this is the right place. I was very small then and he'd always tell me: From tall oaks little acorns grow. And he always rubbed the top of my head when he said it. Just like you were doing.

The Monk has stopped stroking his hair. He now resumes.

Yes, just like that. He took me everywhere with him so that someday when he wasn't around I could make my own way.

Monk: You were born blind, then.

Boy: That's what I was told. But of course I couldn't understand what that meant and I still don't.

Laughs.

My parents, my brothers, my sisters, they all tried to explain to me as I was growing up what it meant to be blind. And what it meant to see. Oh, my, how they tried. But I'm as ignorant as ever. I just can't understand how eyes see. How it's possible to see something without feeling it first.

Monk: And so everyone in your family could see, except for you.

Boy: That's what they told me, Sir.

Smiles.

My mother's eyes, they told me, were blue. The stories they told me trying to make me understand what blue was! Such lovely stories I heard about blue spruce and blue skies and the blue of chimney smoke. I am not one bit closer now to knowing what blue is than I was then but I'll never forget those stories and the sounds of their voices so eager to make me see.

Pause.

And you, Sir, were you also born blind?

Monk: No. I did it myself with a spoon.

Boy: Sir?

Monk: My eyes. I spooned them out. First one then the other.

Boy: You are telling me tales, aren't you, Sir?

Monk: Give me your hand.

The Boy offers his hand. The Monk finds it. Takes off his dark glasses and guides the Boy's hands to his eyes.

Press. Go ahead and press. Don't worry. Press hard. There's nothing there anymore.

Boy: It is not for me to pry as to why you would do such a thing to yourself but I am very sorry that you had your reasons, whatever they may be.

Monk: I killed a man. Without lifting a finger He was trying to kill me, so it was self defense. But then it always is. And always will be. I got tired of seeing the same thing over and over again. The same murders. The same flags. The same battles. The same wars. I have seen enough. Let others look on.

Boy: There is good news, Sir.

The Monk laughs. The Boy smiles, happy to have pleased, but not knowing why.

Monk: The way you say that, Boy. There is good news. The way you say it.

Boy: How do I say it, Sir?

Monk: Like you truly believed your words, that's how. Tell me then. What is the good news?

Boy: From what I've heard, Sir, the forces of freedom are meeting with triumph everywhere. One or two pockets of tyranny still remain but their days are numbered and soon the whole world will be free.

Monk: Free for what?

Boy: Sir?

Monk: FREE FOR WHAT? We could all make a nice long shopping list of free from what we want to be. But free for what? Do you know?

Boy: No, Sir.

Monk: So where's the good news?

Laughs.

When the whole world is free then all the wars we've had up to now will look like the Golden Age of Man. Because then the blood will really flow when the world wide civil wars of liberation from freedom begin.

He reaches out with his hand. Grabs the Boy by his shirt collar and pulls him toward himself.

Listen to me, boy, the only way to stop this endless slaughter is to let life slide until it becomes so worthless and meaningless that it will no longer be worth the effort it takes to take another man's life. Only then will there be peace on earth There's your good news.

He lets go of the Boy. Al has been stifling his coughing for a while and can't stifle it anymore. He coughs. The Monk and the Boy respond to the sound. Get up on their feet. Look around.

Monk: Who's there? If you are robbers we have nothing of value. Nothing.

Angel: We're not going to hurt anybody.

The Monk and the Boy react to the sound of Angel's voice. The Boy feels around with his stick.

Boy: Where are you, Sir?

Al: We're up here.

The new voice causes both the Monk and the Boy to respond in that direction.

Boy: There's two of you?

Angel: Yes, there's two of us. Me and my partner.

The Boy has located the post of the cross with his stick. Feels it now with his hands. He feels higher and higher threatening perhaps to touch Angel's feet.

That's far enough. This is government property.

The Boy pulls his hand back and looks up.

Boy: Excuse me for asking, Sir, but what are you doing up there?

Angel: What do you think we're doing? We're . . . eh . . . we're up here in a kind of a . . . call it eh . . . a . . .

Needs help.

Al: Observation post.

Angel: That's right. That's what it is. It's an observation post.

Al: We keep an eye on things from up here.

Boy: Please, Sir, could you or your partner help us out?

Al: What kind of help did you have in mind?

Boy: It's been such a long time and I've never gone down this mountain by myself. My father always led the way and I always held his hand. The trail is very narrow and winding and I'm ashamed to admit that I'm afraid to try in on my own.

Al and Angel raise their heads and look at the winding trail down the mountainside.

I want to go home, Sir. Maybe some of my brothers and sisters have survived the war and are waiting for me there. Maybe my mother is alive and would love to see that I am well. The gentleman with me could use a home himself. So I was wondering, if it isn't too much trouble, if one of you could take my hand and lead us down as far as the little bridge . . . Can you see a little bridge down there?

Al and Angel look, lifting up their heads as high as they will go.

Angel: I see it. There it is.

The Boy smiles, relieved. Turns to the Monk.

Boy: We're in the right place after all.

Then turns toward Angel and Al.

We would greatly appreciate your assistance, Sir.

Angel and Al look at each other. The Boy waits for a reply.

Sir?

Neither Angel nor Al wants to be the one to reply. Finally Al does.

Al: I'm afraid we can't do that.

Boy: You can't, Sir?

Al: No. We're not allowed to leave our posts.

Boy: Not even for an hour?

Al: Not even for a second.

Angel: Sorry. If we could we would but as it is . . .

Boy: I understand, Sir. Orders are orders, after all.

We better be going, Sir. I'll do the best I can.

Monk: I'm sure you will, son.

They start to go, the Boy leading, feeling with his stick. The Monk follows.

Al: Wait. Wait a minute.

The Boy and the Monk stop. Angel, puzzled, looks at Al. A beat of silence.

I'm thinking.

Al cranes his neck, taking in the trail that leads

down the mountainside.

I can see a good portion of the trail from here and my partner can probably see the part that I can't.

Angel cranes his neck and looks.

Angel: I see it alright.

Al: So here's what we'll do. We'll guide you along from here. If we shout loudly enough, you'll hear us. Just do what we tell you.

Angel: That's a brilliant idea, Al. That is one brilliant idea. I never would've though of it.

Al: Off you go. But go slowly. Are you ready?

Boy: Yes, Sir. I am. And thank you ever so much.

Al: The trail is about two yards to your right.

As Al gives instructions, the Boy executes them and the Monk follows the Boy.

That's it. Now straight ahead until you hear from one of us. That's it. That's right.

The Boy and the Monk exit. Angel and Al keep their eyes on them. There is a sense that as the trail twists and turns it does so directly in front of them so that when they're shouting their instructions they're looking out at the audience. Each time they shout it costs them much pain. They're shouting their lives away.

Angel: Last thing I expected in a place like this was visitors.

Al: Me too.

Angel: Sure was nice. LEFT! THAT'S IT! NO! NO! KEEP LEFT! THAT'S RIGHT!

Overcomes his pain as he turns to Al.

I gotta hand it to you, Al. You really came through. This was a brilliant solution. Sometimes you intellectuals . . .

Al: RIGHT NOW! SHARP RIGHT! SHARP! ALL THE WAY AROUND! THAT'S IT! NOW STRAIGHT AHEAD!

Angel: How about that kid, eh?

Al: A wonderful boy.

Angel: So polite and all. Sir, this. Sir, that. Thank you, Sir.

Al: He wasn't merely polite. You know how you sometimes get these polite types, but there's no substance to them.

Angel: Are you kidding? The kid's a champ. A

champ, I tell you. LEFT! EASY NOW! THAT'S RIGHT! Not much meat on him, but sinewy. And he had this thing . . . for a kid his age . . . he had this . . .

Al: Poise.

Angel: That's it. He had poise. That's what it was.

Al: RI . . .

He stops in midshout. A little smile.

He did it himself.

Angel: Yeah. Look at him go. His stride is getting longer.

Al: It's all coming back to him now.

A touch of sorrow.

I don't think he needs us anymore.

Angel: The kid's a champ. That's all there is to it. Does your heart good to see a kid like that again.

Al: Yes, it does.

Silence. No longer needed as guides their focus shifts. They relax their vigil. Check in with each other. They're both in a lot of pain. Their breathing is labored.

Angel: How's it going, bro?

Al: There's these black spots in front of my eyes. It's hard to see. What about you?

Angel: I can't feel my legs anymore but the rest hurts real bad. It's like I'm slowly being torn in half. Like a sheet of paper.

Al: Can you see the Kid?

Angel looks out.

Angel: Yeah. He's moving right along.

Smiles at the sight.

Al: It's like the night is falling. I know it's not. I know for a fact that you're crucified but what I see is something else. I see a man with his arms open wide as if he were ready to embrace the world. You look like a masterpiece, my friend.

Silence. Angel has no reply he can make.

Angel: Do you think we should convert to something before we die?

Al: Convert to what?

Angel: I don't know. Something.

Al: Do you believe in something?

Angel: Not that I know of.

Al: Then what're you going to convert to?

Angel: Is that how it works? You have to believe in something ahead of time.

Al: Of course. Why else would you convert to it?

Angel: Good point. There goes that idea.

Silence. Angel looks out. Smiles.

They're about to cross the bridge.

Al looks out.

Al: I can't see the bridge.

Angel: Oh, Al!

Al: What? What?

Angel: You should see our boy.

Al: Oh yeah? What's he doing?

Angel: He's stopped in the middle of the bridge and he's waving to us. He's just standing there waving.

In the direction of the Boy. Softly.

Goodbye.

Al: I doubt he can hear you.

Angel: I know but . . .

Al: Is he still there?

Angel: Yes. Still waving.

Al: He probably wants to hear from us. Wants to be sure that we see he's made it safely. So we don't worry.

Angel: I think you're right, Al.

Al: We should let him know then, right?

Angel: Right.

Al: Are you ready, Angel?

Angel: I'm as ready as I'll ever be, Al.

Al: Then here we go.

He gathers himself.

GOOD-BYE!

Angel: GOOD-BYE!

Both: GOOD-BYE! GOOD-BYE!

Each good-bye costs them. The pain is enormous but they manage to overcome the pain and to enter a state of ecstasy. It is no longer just to the Boy that they're shouting their good-byes. It's to each other, the audience, to the light that's dimming, to the shores of the known world they are leaving.

Both: GOOD-BYE! GOOD-BYE! GOOD-BYE . . .

The lights dim and out.

THE END.

SQUARE ONE
A Play by Steve Tesich

The Oscar-winning author of *Breaking Away*

With *Square One,* Steve Tesich once again moves us further onto a frightening frontier of the twentieth century. He discovers the brutal social rhythms of conformity as they rise up to silence the unique impulses and creative reflexes of modern man. While most contemporary dramatists are content to putter around their neighbors' gardens in order to sniff out the garden variety of domestic calamity, Tesich creates a highly sophisticated hybrid of contemporary existence to give us a terrifying whiff of the future.

"An achingly sad, brutal, futuristic comedy that is strangely sweet as often as it is chilling."
—Linda Winer, NEWSDAY

"The most memorable play to hit off-Broadway this season." —John Harris, THEATERWEEK

"A brave new world where nothing is particularly brave or particularly new. . . . IT IS A WARNING. Do see it. I suspect you owe it to yourself and somehow to our communal future."
—Clive Barnes, NEW YORK POST

Steve Tesich is the author of many plays including *Division Street* and *The Speed of Darkness*. He won the Academy Award for Best Screenplay for *Breaking Away*. He divides his time between Manhattan and Colorado.

paper • ISBN: 1-55783-076-2

APPLAUSE